# CAREERS IN SEARCH AND RESCUE OPERATIONS

CAREERS IN
# EMERGENCY MEDICAL RESPONSE TEAMS'
SEARCH AND RESCUE UNITS

## Jeri Freedman

the rosen publishing group's

**rosen central**

*To my father, Lee Freedman, with love*

Published in 2003 by The Rosen Publishing Group, Inc.
29 East 21st Street, New York, NY 10010

**Library of Congress Cataloging-in-Publication Data**

Freedman, Jeri.
Careers in emergency medical response teams' search and rescue units / Jeri Freedman.
    p. cm. — (Careers in search and rescue operations)
Includes bibliographical references and index.
ISBN 0-8239-3831-X 26.50)
1. Rescue work—Vocational guidance. 2. Disaster medicine—Vocational guidance. 3. Emergency medical services—Vocational guidance.
I. Title. II. Series.
RA645.9 .F74 2003
616.02'5'023—dc21

                                                          2002013341

*Manufactured in the United States of America*

# CONTENTS

# INTRODUCTION

## When Disaster Strikes

At 8:45 AM on September 11, 2001, terrorists flew a hijacked Boeing 767 into the north tower of the World Trade Center in New York City. At 9:03 AM, a second plane struck the south tower. Less than an hour later, the south tower collapsed, followed shortly by the north tower. In Arlington, Virginia, just outside Washington, D.C., at 9:43 AM, a third plane crashed into the Pentagon. A fourth plane crashed in a field in rural Pennsylvania, at 10:10 AM.

In Washington, Tommy Thompson, secretary of the U.S. Department of Health and Human Services, activated the National Disaster Medical System. For the first time ever, all eighty of the emergency medical assistance teams that participate in the program were called up. As a result, emergency medical assistance teams from the New York and Washington areas went into action immediately. Soon after, they were joined by additional emergency medical response (EMR) teams from all over the country.

The New York teams set up a field hospital a short distance from the World Trade Center. Emergency medical personnel were also dispatched from New Jersey to the World Trade Center site and other locations in New York and New Jersey that were being set up for emergency medical treatment. At the ferry terminal in nearby Hoboken, New Jersey, as well as at other sites along the

In Arlington, Virginia, EMR workers establish a medical triage station a safe distance away from the Pentagon, which is still emitting clouds of black smoke after the terrorist attacks on September 11, 2001.

New Jersey waterfront, temporary medical areas were set up to treat huge numbers of victims arriving from New York by Coast Guard boats and ferries. These victims were treated by medical personnel and, when necessary, transported to hospitals in New York and New Jersey. Several thousand people were treated for injuries at the temporary medical facilities and at New York City hospitals. According to Mary Ann Littel in "First Response to Terror," which appeared in the University of Medicine and Dentistry of New Jersey's *HealthState*, approximately 20,000 people were seen, triaged (sorted by severity of injury), taken to hospitals, or decontaminated (sprayed to remove debris) by emergency medical personnel on the New Jersey waterfront.

The emergency medical response teams included doctors, nurses, emergency medical technicians, and other medical personnel. They worked tirelessly to treat the wounded and see that those who were seriously hurt got safely to facilities where they could receive further medical care.

September 11 is perhaps the most dramatic example of emergency medical response teams at work. There are many types of emergencies in which these brave men and women save lives. This book will explore the nature of emergency medical response work, the requirements for the job, and the different types of work available in this exciting field. How emergency medical response teams respond to major search and rescue operations and disasters such as the events of September 11 is discussed in chapter 6.

# CHAPTER 1

# Life on the Front Lines

When disaster strikes, EMR teams provide frontline emergency medical care, life support, and transportation to hospitals. They rescue and treat people who have had life-threatening heart, asthma, or other disease-related attacks; those who have been injured in accidents; and those who are the victims of natural or man-made disasters. Among other duties, members of EMR teams perform cardiopulmonary resuscitation (CPR), which keeps blood and oxygen moving through a person's body; restart the hearts of patients whose hearts have stopped; provide respiratory care (help people who are having trouble breathing); deliver babies; splint broken legs; dress wounds; treat burns and allergic reactions; and transport patients to hospitals. EMR teams treat the victims of car accidents, the victims of gunshot wounds at crime scenes, and those who become injured in cave-ins or building collapses as other emergency services personnel free

In upstate New York, an auto accident involving multiple vehicles is staged during fire department EMT training. Even though people who want to be EMTs must undergo extensive training courses, nothing can prepare them for what they will see while on the job.

them. They work in busy cities, large industrial complexes, remote rural communities, and isolated wilderness areas.

EMR workers are employed by ambulance services, hospitals, police and fire departments, wilderness rescue teams, and the military. According to the U.S. Bureau of Labor Statistics, in 2000 there were 172,000 emergency medical technicians (EMTs). Out of every ten EMTs, four work for private ambulance services; three work for fire departments, public ambulance services, or other public emergency medical services (EMSs); two work for hospitals (either in the facility or as part of ambulance crews); and one works in any of a number of other industries that employ EMTs, such as wilderness rescue or industrial safety.

## The EMS Team

Emergency medical services are organizations that provide urgently needed medical care and patient transportation. The EMS team includes the following:

- **Emergency medical dispatcher (EMD):** EMDs receive calls from people who are in emergency situations. They obtain information about the nature of the problem and the location of the patient, prioritize the calls according to how severe the emergency is, send (dispatch) the emergency medical team, and tell the caller how to handle the situation until the EMS team arrives.

- **EMS-trained first responders:** These include firefighters, police officers, and other people who work for public agencies or private companies that provide emergency care on the scene until EMTs arrive.

- **Medical director:** Every EMS team includes a doctor who is based at a hospital or other facility. The medical director recommends treatments to the EMTs on-site. He or she also approves the medicine given and medical procedures performed by EMTs on patients.

- **Emergency medical technicians:** EMTs are trained to provide emergency medical services to victims and to transport patients to medical facilities. When a medical emergency occurs, it is EMTs who usually provide the most immediate response.

## Why Be an EMT?

According to the U.S. Department of Labor, the demand for EMTs is expected to increase faster than most professions through at least 2010. This is mainly because the population is growing and the size of cities and towns is increasing. EMTs can work either full- or part-time, and there are a variety of schedules available. Because of this flexibility, it is an excellent career for someone who does not want a regular nine-to-five job.

## The Star of Life

The symbol of EMS is the Star of Life. It was designed in 1973 by Leo R. Schwartz, who was EMS branch chief at the National Highway Traffic Safety Administration. It is a six-pointed star created by crossing three bars, with a snake coiled around the center bar. According to an article by Arline Zatz in *Rescue-EMS Magazine*, the six points of the star stand for the six basic types of services provided by EMS. These are detection, reporting, response, on-scene care, care in transit, and transfer to definitive care. The snake coiled around the center bar stands for the staff of Asclepius, the Greek god of healing, and it is also part of the symbol used by physicians.

Working as an EMT offers the satisfaction of helping people and providing a vitally needed service. At the same time, it is a varied and often exciting career. As with firefighters, police officers, and military personnel, a sense of camaraderie often develops among members of an EMR team as they work together closely in demanding situations.

# CHAPTER 2

## The History of EMR

The history of emergency medical treatment is closely tied to war. In ancient Rome, older soldiers were sometimes assigned to move the wounded from battlefields for treatment. During the Middle Ages, members of religious orders would treat the wounded (often from opposing sides) on battlefields. For example, the Benedictine monks who made up the Knights Hospitalers of the Order of St. John of Jerusalem treated those who were wounded in the Crusades.

Baron Dominique-Jean Larrey, surgeon in chief of the French army during the Napoleonic Wars, is credited with creating the first army medical corps in 1792. This unit treated soldiers on the front lines and transported them back to field hospitals. Larrey is also credited with being the first person to assign specific vehicles for transporting the wounded. Small, fast, and easily maneuverable horse-drawn carts—usually used to move mobile cannons—were converted and were called ambulances.

The first use of ambulances to transport injured civilians to hospitals dates back to the end of the American Civil War. When those who had provided this type of service to soldiers on the battlefield returned to their communities, they continued to use the skills they had gained in wartime—only now they transported civilian patients to local hospitals. The first hospital-based ambulance service in the United States was established in 1865 by the Commercial Hospital of Cincinnati (later Cincinnati General).

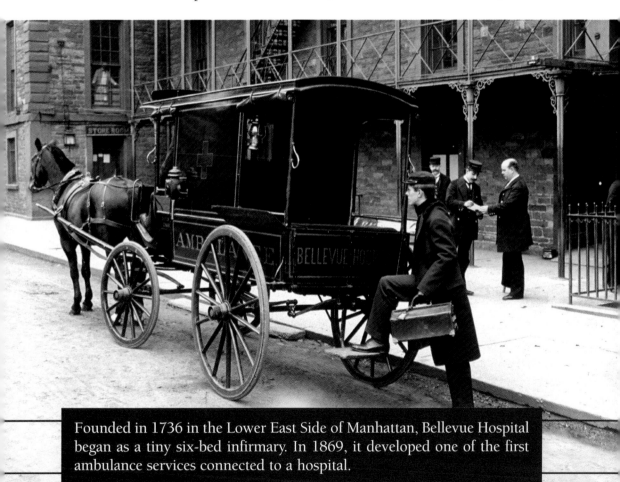

Founded in 1736 in the Lower East Side of Manhattan, Bellevue Hospital began as a tiny six-bed infirmary. In 1869, it developed one of the first ambulance services connected to a hospital.

In Canada, the city of Toronto established a municipal ambulance service as early as 1883. It was operated by the Toronto Department of Public Health and consisted of two horse-drawn vehicles. A motorized ambulance was used as early as 1899 at Michael Reese Hospital in Chicago. Motorized ambulances were used on a larger scale in France during World War I, when volunteers, such as those in the American Ambulance Field Service, transported injured soldiers from the front to field hospitals. St. John's Ambulance service conducted the first formal training for ambulance attendants for the Toronto police in 1892. In the United States, the first formal EMS unit was formed in Roanoke, Virginia, during the 1920s by Julian Stanley Wise. There were some motorized ambulances early in the twentieth century. However, in both the United States and Canada, more than half of all patients in need of emergency care were taken to hospitals by funeral home and mortuary vehicles well into the first half of the twentieth century.

## The History of Medical Airlift

According to Treg Manning in *The Helicopter in Air Medical Services*, the first use of air ambulances dates back to 1870 during the siege of Paris by the Prussians, when balloons were used to rescue over 100 soldiers. A number of officials and physicians suggested using airplanes to transport the wounded in France in World War I. It was not until 1923, however, that airlifts were officially recognized as a means of moving the injured from battlefields and were written into the Geneva Convention, which is a series of international rules governing the conduct of wars. In 1925, the U.S. Army Air Corps created the first medical section of the corps. The first use of a helicopter for medical purposes occurred in 1943, when one was used to fly plasma to sailors wounded in an explosion on the U.S. Navy destroyer *Turner*, off the coast of New Jersey. Helicopters were first used to transport the wounded during the Korean War.

According to Manning, Bill Mathews, a businessman in Etna, California, was the first person to attempt to start a helicopter

U.S. troops cross a plank bridge over marshy ground as they carry wounded South Korean soldiers to a helicopter, where they will be airlifted to safety.

service. However, helicopters did not become a common form of emergency medical transportation until the 1970s, when the need for good civilian emergency medical services was finally addressed by the U.S. Department of Transportation.

## Addressing the Need for EMS at Home

During the Vietnam War, medical researchers claimed that a soldier injured on the battlefield had a better chance of survival than a person injured in a traffic accident at home. It was

This burn victim is being tended to on the streets of Springfield, Massachusetts. Although first- and second-degree burns are often very painful, they are seldom fatal.

decided that an organized method of treating civilian victims of trauma was needed. The U.S. National Academy of Sciences published a report in 1966 titled "Accidental Death and Disability: The Neglected Disease of Modern Society." The report called attention to the lack of emergency medical services, including the necessity for an efficient way to transport patients in need of emergency care to hospitals.

In 1966, Congress enacted (made into law) legislation that created the National Highway Traffic Safety Administration (NHTSA), which in turn established federal standards for emergency medical services. The Department of Transportation decided to use what the military had learned to create a more effective civilian emergency medical response system. This included making standards for EMTs, who could provide emergency medical treatment on-site. In 1973, the EMS Systems Act was passed by Congress. This act provided additional funding for EMS services. In 1975, the official designation of paramedic was established, and paramedics were trained to provide advanced life support, including using equipment to assist patients to breathe and heart monitors. In 1990, Congress passed the Trauma Care Systems Planning and Development Act to encourage the development of statewide systems for dealing with trauma.

In the wake of the events of September 11, 2001, many communities have reviewed existing plans or created new ones for dealing with emergency medical disasters on a large scale, and it is likely that emergency medical response systems will continue to evolve.

# CHAPTER 3

## Training for the Challenge

As a member of an EMR team, you will be confronted with people in life-threatening situations who depend on you to rescue them and provide medical treatment. You must be able to handle the stress of dealing with frightened and upset people at the scenes of disasters and accidents. In addition, providing emergency medical assistance may require you to enter areas where there is debris from the wreckage of a vehicle, or where access is difficult because of rough terrain or bad weather.

## What It Takes to Be an EMT

EMTs must lift and carry heavy people and objects. They must be in good physical shape and be able to work under physically demanding conditions for long periods of time. They must be observant and make good decisions quickly. In addition to all the other skills required to be a good EMT, EMTs who drive ambulances must be able to reach the scene of an emergency

An ambulance waits while medics remove the owner of this sport utility vehicle from the driver's seat. The SUV crashed after colliding with a pickup truck just outside of Jacksonville, Mississippi.

quickly but without endangering themselves or other people on the road. For this reason, EMT drivers take special courses in ambulance driving.

### Patient Interaction Skills

The key to success for an EMT is to be dependable, to exercise good judgment, and to care about people. An EMT must be able to remain calm and treat distressed patients and family members with patience and courtesy while dealing with the urgent need for medical treatment. It is also important for an EMT to maintain a neat and professional appearance and behave in a professional manner. Finally, it is necessary that an EMT listen sympathetically to patients and others involved in emergency situations.

### Diagnosis and Treatment Skills

EMTs need a thorough knowledge of anatomy and the basic procedures required to treat a wide range of injuries. Basic medical treatment is taught in EMT courses. However, it is up to the individual EMTs to make sure their knowledge is current. EMTs also need to be familiar with the proper use of equipment and the protocols, or rules, they should be following for treating various types of emergency medical problems. These protocols are usually provided by the organizations that employ the EMTs. It is vital that such procedures be carried out correctly for the safety of both the patient and the EMT.

It is very important that an EMT remain up to date on the latest information and technology in the field. EMTs can take continuing medical education (CME) workshops, read news-letters and magazines devoted to EMR, such as *EMS Magazine*, and participate in organizations such as the National Association of Emergency Medical Technicians.

## Becoming an EMT

To obtain certification, an EMT must have knowledge of a num-ber of different skills. These include how to use and maintain equipment; how to assess and diagnose patients; how to move patients; how to provide various types of medical treatment, including basic procedures such as how to keep a patient's airway open so he or she can breathe; giving medicine; performing CPR; and following proper safety procedures. In addition, an EMT must have effective communication skills—verbal and written (for writing reports).

In both the United States and Canada there are various levels of EMTs. In the 1990s, the NHTSA adopted the National Emergency Medical Services Education and Practice Blueprint. This is a series of standards that was developed as the result of the combined efforts of EMS practitioners in a range of national organizations, including the following: the National Association of State Directors, the American Academy of Pediatrics, the National Council of State EMS Training

Coordinators, the National Association of Emergency Medical Services Physicians, the American College of Emergency Physicians, the American Ambulance Association, the National Registry of EMTs, the U.S. Fire Administration, the International Association of Fire Chiefs, the National Association of Emergency Medical Technicians, the Emergency Nurse Association, the American College of Surgeons, the U.S. Department of Defense, and the U.S. Department of Health and Human Services. Although in the United States, requirements for EMT certification differ from state to state, the blueprint defines the basic criteria for EMT certification.

## Levels of Certification

Under this standard, there are three levels of EMT certification. EMT-Basics (also called EMT-1 or EMT-Ambulance) can check pulse rates and blood pressure, treat shock victims, dress wounds, perform CPR, and deliver babies. EMT-Intermediates (EMT-2 and EMT-3) can use devices that help people breathe, set up IVs (devices that deliver medication and fluids into a patient's vein), and use a device called a defibrillator to administer a shock to restart a patient's stopped heart. EMT-Paramedics (EMT-4) can give medication and use advanced life-support equipment such as heart monitors.

To become an EMT-Basic you must take 100 to 120 hours of classroom training and serve a ten-hour internship in an emergency room. Certification courses are available at a variety of

At this EMT training session, a cardiopulmonary resuscitation (CPR) dummy is used by trainees to practice on. A simple method that can save lives, CPR is taught all over the world.

colleges and universities, and in many areas, training is also offered by the police, fire, and health departments. To advance from EMT-Basic to higher levels requires additional classroom training and on-the-job experience. In the United States, individual states have exams to certify EMTs. In addition, the National Registry of Emergency Medical Technicians is an organization that issues written and practical exams for EMT qualification on a national level. This makes it easier for EMTs to carry their certification to another state if they move. EMD certification is also available for emergency medical dispatchers.

In Canada, there are also several levels of EMTs. The exact designations of EMTs vary from province to province (or territory). For instance, British Columbia uses the designations EMA-I (emergency medical assistant I), EMA-II, and EMA-III, while New Brunswick uses the terms Basic EMT and Intermediate EMT. The responsibilities of the different levels of EMTs in Canada are similar to those in the United States. In December 2001, the Canadian Association of Emergency Physicians submitted a proposal to the Commission on the Future of Health Care in Canada suggesting that national standards be established for pre-hospital and emergency medical services in Canada. Among other things, it proposes the establishment of national standards for the different levels of paramedic training. In Canada, the Paramedic Association of Canada (PAC) represents EMTs involved in providing emergency medical services.

# CHAPTER 4

## Saving Lives

In an article titled "On-Scene Care (Trauma!)" in *RN* magazine, Pamela Stacey tells this story from her first day of EMT training: Her teacher said, "You're driving down a rural road and see a car swerving back and forth across the center line. It hits a patch of ice, spins out of control, and strikes a utility pole. There's no one else in sight, and the closest house is a mile down the road. You stop. What's the first thing you check?" Pamela blurted out, "Level of consciousness." "Wrong," the teacher said. "You check to see if the scene is safe."

### Facing Danger on the Job

One of the most important things that EMS personnel do when answering an emergency call is to ensure that they, the patient, and any bystanders, are safe. Although being an EMT can be exciting, it can also be dangerous. Before venturing out to help people on search and rescue missions, EMTs need to check out

A woman in isolation gear (*right*) is escorted out of her Florida home by a member of the Broward County Fire Rescue Hazardous Materials team. The rescue team was worried that the woman had been exposed to deadly anthrax spores.

the scene for hazards. These may include dangerous debris, oncoming vehicles, loose electrical wires, or hazardous chemicals. EMTs may also encounter people fighting, people abusing drugs or alcohol, people with weapons, and sometimes even pets who mistakenly think that the EMT approaching their master is a threat.

How do you avoid danger on the job? First, you need to be aware of everything happening around you. Then, examine the surroundings for signs of danger, either from people or natural sources, such as vehicles or falling pieces of damaged buildings. Use your nose, too, to detect smells that might mean danger such as leaking chemicals or smoke. When EMTs sense danger, they first use cover, which means putting obstacles between themselves and the source of the danger. Second, they use portable radios to contact the appropriate authorities such as firefighters or police officers, whose job it is to deal with the danger. Sometimes, in certain types of urban rescue situations such as when working at crime scenes with the police, EMTs wear bulletproof vests or other types of protective gear.

## Rescuing the Wounded

After making sure that the scene is safe, the next thing EMTs do is figure out exactly what happened to cause the emergency situation. For example, at the scene of an accident, an EMT will try to figure out how an injury occurred. If a person has been injured by a weapon, the EMTs try to figure out what type of weapon was used. If a person was injured in a fall, they try to estimate how far that person has fallen. All these things help them establish the best type of treatment. When treating a patient, EMTs put on protective gear such as gloves or masks to guard against germs. If there is more than one patient, the EMTs may need to call for backup.

When dealing with a conscious patient, the first thing the EMTs do is introduce themselves. Next, they do an initial assessment of the patient to see if he or she is alert and able to talk sensibly. Then they check the patient's vital signs (pulse and heart rate, for instance), which can give an idea of the patient's general condition. They also check for signs of trauma such as bleeding. They then ask the patient questions that may reveal useful information, such as what his or her symptoms are and any background health information that may be relevant.

## Treating the Injured

EMTs must administer medical treatment under the direction of a doctor. If, for example, it is necessary to administer medication, the EMTs call their physician contact, who must approve the administration of medication. In addition to this direct contact with a medical director, EMTs may rely on documents that provide guidelines for how to handle patients in an emergency. These documents, called protocols, are provided by the organization that the EMTs

## Bronchospasm Protocol

1. Assess the patient and check vital signs and level of consciousness.
2. Make sure the patient meets the criteria for treatment (for example, the patient is over one year old and is not allergic to the medication; these criteria are listed at the start of the protocol).
3. Make sure the patient is in the correct position for treatment.
4. Administer the medication salbutamol using a mask.
5. Reassess the patient for signs that the medication is working and for any negative effects of the medication.
6. Administer a second dose if required.
7. Transport the patient.
8. Monitor the patient during transportation.
9. Notify the medical facility about the patient's condition and the medication given.

work for. For example, the above is a simplified version of a protocol produced by the provincial government of Manitoba for EMTs treating a patient with asthma. (Manitoba's EMS protocols are listed on its Web site at http://www.gov.mb.ca/health/ems/protocols/index.html.)

## Transporting Patients

After the EMTs provide emergency on-site treatment, they transport the patient to the hospital. On the way to the hospital, EMTs provide the basic treatment necessary to ensure that the patient

EMS workers crowd around a Wisconsin man who was struck by a train. The man was kept in stable condition until a helicopter could airlift him to a Milwaukee hospital.

arrives in as good shape as possible. During transport, the EMTs again check the patient's vital signs. In the case of a seriously ill or injured patient, this reassessment may be performed over and over again every few minutes. The EMTs radio the hospital, reporting on the patient's state and response to any treatment given. Once they arrive at the hospital, they not only turn the patient over to the staff there, but also tell the hospital personnel who receive the patient about his or her symptoms, status, and any treatment that has been given, as well as information about the nature of the incident that led to the patient's injury.

Once the emergency is over, emergency medical response personnel are required to write reports about the incidents they responded to. These include a pre-hospital care report, which lists important information about the patient's symptoms, condition, and care prior to arriving at the hospital. This serves several purposes: It provides information to the hospital that is receiving the patient, it helps emergency medical personnel learn how to respond successfully to specific types of emergencies, and it helps the government keep track of statistics on the kinds of accidents that occur.

## The EMT's Equipment

The largest piece of equipment an EMT has is the ambulance itself. Small ambulances—similar in size to standard vans—are frequently used for first-response units of organizations like the

## The EMTs' Equipment

Many different types of equipment used by EMTs are carried in today's ambulances. Equipment commonly used in EMR includes:

• **Equipment for patient comfort, protection, and infection control**: general supplies such as masks, gloves, blankets, and restraining devices for controlling unruly patients such as those on drugs.

• **Patient transfer equipment**: a wheeled ambulance stretcher, a folding stair chair (in which a patient can be seated and carried down stairs), and specialized stretchers used for purposes such as removing an immobile patient from a location inaccessible to an ordinary stretcher.

• **Respiratory equipment**: equipment to help a patient breathe, such as ventilation masks and airway tubes for children and adults, portable oxygen delivery systems, and oxygen cylinders.

• **Cardiac equipment**: Ambulances that carry paramedics may carry portable cardiac resuscitation equipment such as defibrillators, which are used to restart a patient's heart if it stops beating.

- **Immobilization equipment**: items such as splints, spine boards, and neck collars to support patients who may have broken bones.

- **Wound care supplies**: bandages, wound and burn dressings, and related supplies.

- **Emergency childbirth supplies**: items for use in delivering babies, and supplies such as blankets and caps to keep the newborn baby warm.

- **Supplies for treatment of poisoning**: items such as activated charcoal to counteract oral poisonings and equipment for cleaning a patient's eyes with water.

- **Safety equipment**: items used to help ensure the safety of the EMTs themselves such as a portable radio, identification vests (which allow other emergency personnel at the site of an incident to identify the EMTs), flares, jumper cables, binoculars, a pry bar and other tools, utility rope, and personal protection gear such as gloves, helmets, and goggles for eye protection during rescue operations. In extremely hazardous situations, EMTs may use special clothing such as fireproof pants or steel-toed shoes.

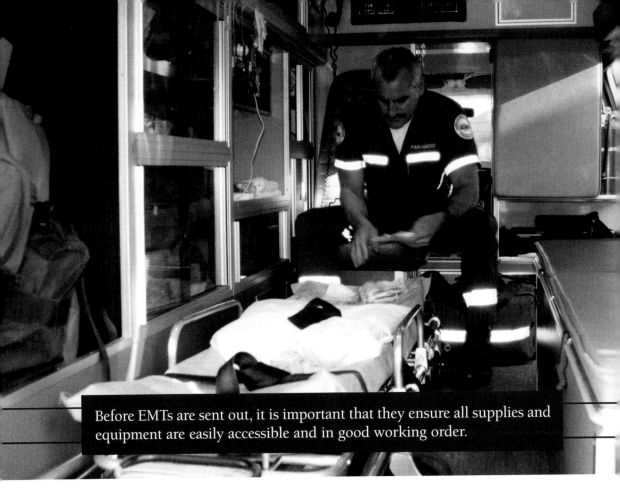

Before EMTs are sent out, it is important that they ensure all supplies and equipment are easily accessible and in good working order.

police and fire services. However, beginning in the 1990s, it became common to include special equipment in ambulances such as advanced medical monitoring devices for use in emergency rescue operations. Equipment storage and work areas have also become larger. Because of the weight of this additional equipment, ambulances have become heavier and more rugged.

After each call, the EMTs clean all the equipment used on the call. Then, they must restock any items that were used, like oxygen tanks and dressings. Finally, they make up the stretcher so that it is ready to use in the next emergency.

# CHAPTER 5

## EMR Special Operations

Emergency medical response personnel work in a wide variety of environments, ranging from inner cities to the wilderness, and different types of organizations. Some EMTs work in special operations. These include EMT pilots and EMTs who work on flight rescue teams such as Life Flight, those who are part of wilderness rescue teams, and those who are part of police, fire, and military services.

There are a number of types of special operations teams—ice rescue, hazardous-materials rescue, heavy industrial rescue, urban rescue, water (surface and underwater) rescue, vehicle rescue, and wilderness rescue—that exist within EMR. The EMTs who are part of such teams receive additional training in their special area in addition to regular EMT training.

## Airlift Services

Sometimes it is necessary to transport a patient to a hospital by air. Such transportation may be made by either helicopter or airplane. Patients may need to be transported by air if they are very badly hurt and the nearest hospital is too far away to reach in a timely fashion; if they are rescued from a wilderness area where there is no medical facility; if they need to be taken to a special type of medical facility that is too far away to reach quickly by ground transport, such as a burn treatment

Sometimes the closest hospital lacks the equipment or specialists to handle a patient's injuries. To get the patient to a facility that can treat him or her, EMTs often load the patient onto an air ambulance.

center; or if weather conditions, such as blizzards or floods, make driving too hazardous.

EMTs employed by airlift services must be certified paramedics. They must have three years of ground-based EMT experience before becoming air EMTs. Because they deal with very seriously ill patients, air EMTs are required to have training in advanced life-support procedures and devices such as equipment used to monitor the way a patient's heart is beating or to keep a patient breathing. The pilots of emergency airlift planes and helicopters are EMTs as well as pilots.

## Wilderness Rescue

EMTs are employed by ski patrols and park services as well as by mountain, water, air, and disaster relief services involved in wilderness rescue. According to the Mountain Rescue Association (MRA), most wilderness rescue in the United States is the responsibility of the sheriff's department in a given area, although in some locations, it is handled by the state police or the fish and game department.

Canada has a national search and rescue program that is divided into three areas: air, sea, and ground. The Canadian Coast Guard is responsible for sea searches and marine vessels, and the Department of Canadian Heritage is responsible for ground search and rescue in national parks, conservation areas, and historic sites. The police forces of Canadian provinces and territories are responsible for ground search and rescue services in their local areas, and the Royal Canadian Mounted Police are active in this as well.

Generally, the members of rescue teams practice as a group and undergo special training in wilderness rescue. In addition to medical expertise, members of such teams are trained in wilderness skills such as tracking, land navigation, using search techniques to locate lost persons, and skills needed in the type of environment in which the team works, such as wildfire control, mountain climbing, or water rescue. Some search and rescue teams use experts with specially trained dogs to locate trapped or injured people in remote areas. Wilderness-type rescue training is also required for those engaged in urban "trench" rescues (when street trenches collapse with workers in them) because this type of rescue requires skills similar to those used to rescue people from wilderness trench disasters.

Wilderness rescue teams can be certified by the MRA. To become certified, the team must pass tests in rugged terrain search, technical rope rescue in a wilderness environment, and alpine (snow, ice, and high-altitude) rescue. Wilderness rescue team workers must be in excellent condition since they may have to gain access to remote locations, move and lift heavy objects and people, and carry heavy packs and equipment for long distances over rough terrain.

### Treating Victims in the Wilderness

Victims of environmental emergencies can experience special problems because of exposure to heat or cold. Normally, no matter how hot or cold it is where people live, the body regulates its temperature so that it stays at 98.6 degrees Fahrenheit. If, however, a person is exposed to extreme heat or cold for an extended period of time, he or she may suffer serious medical problems. EMTs working in wilderness rescue must be prepared to treat temperature-related problems such as frostbite.

Emergency medical personnel involved in wilderness rescue often rely on special wilderness protocols for treating medical emergencies. In a non-wilderness situation, the goal of EMTs is to provide the minimum amount of treatment needed to ensure that the patient can be safely transported to a hospital, and then to transport the patient. In the wilderness, however, it may be impossible to reach a medical facility quickly. Therefore, wilderness protocols provide procedures for more extensive care that EMTs may need to provide when it will take longer than two hours to reach a hospital. For example, EMTs do not usually fix dislocated bones. Instead, they transport the patient to a hospital, where treatment is given. However, if a patient does not receive treatment for several hours, he or she may suffer permanent damage. Because of this, in a wilderness rescue situation, the EMT may have to provide such treatment in the field.

## Police Department EMTs

Some police departments employ EMTs who are also trained police officers. These officers carry a limited amount of emergency medical equipment in their police cars. Most often, they act as first responders—that is, they are the first to arrive and treat victims at accident scenes or perform CPR in the event of emergencies. Job benefits are often very good for police EMTs. However, working as a police EMT can be more dangerous than working as an ambulance-based EMT since your skills will often be used at the crime scenes.

## Fire Department EMTs

In addition to fighting fires, fire departments often deal with natural disasters and accidents involving hazardous materials. Fire department EMTs treat the victims at the sites of such accidents and fires, as well as provide traditional emergency services in areas that do not have independent emergency medical services. EMTs who work for fire departments perform many of the same tasks as those employed by public or private ambulance services. In addition, however, EMTs employed by fire departments are trained as firefighters. They may work in ambulances or they may be part of the crew on the fire truck, in which case, some medical equipment will be carried on the truck to allow the EMT to perform basic emergency treatment on-site until a regular ambulance arrives.

## Industrial EMTs

Some industrial companies employ EMTs on-site in case their employees have an accident with the machines they are working with. Also, some companies that work with or produce hazardous materials employ EMTs on-site in case of an industrial accident such as leakage of a chemical or toxic gas. This type of accident can affect both workers at the plant and people living or working nearby.

These Swiss rescue workers have carefully flown far up into the mountains to rescue three skiers trapped in an avalanche. Many situations that rescue workers find themselves in contain real elements of danger.

EMTs in such positions can often predict the types of accidents most likely to occur and can thus be prepared to deal with them. For example, Dow Chemical Company's Texas chemical production facility maintains an emergency response staff of eighty-five people that provides security, fire, and emergency medical services, complete with its own dispatch center for coordinating emergency response. Although the emergency medical staff deals mostly with on-site medical emergencies, they are trained to respond to larger-scale industrial emergencies such as a chemical leak or explosion. Such on-site EMS teams are especially important in large industrial or chemical plants that are located in rural areas, where the emergency medical services may be small or rely on volunteers.

## Native American EMTs

Some EMTs provide emergency medical services to particular populations. For example, the National Native American EMS Association (NNAEMSA) is a group of seventy programs that provide EMS services specifically to Native Americans, both on and off reservations. According to NNAEMSA, they provide care for more than 500,000 Native Americans every year. The organizations that make up NNAEMSA often provide services to populations that may have difficulty in obtaining care from other EMS services because of their remoteness or the difficulty imposed by the terrain in which they live. For instance, Maniilaq EMS at the

## The Lighter Side of EMR

Often the producers of large events such as rock concerts and sporting events hire EMTs to be on hand in case there is a medical emergency. Sometimes such EMTs find themselves in unusual situations. According to "Along for the Ride," an article by Melissa Phillips in *Airman's World*, a group of medics from the 90th Medical Group of the 187th Aeroevacuation Squadron of the Wyoming Air National Guard in Cheyenne, Wyoming, have volunteered their services at the Frontier Days rodeo in Cheyenne since the 1940s. The medics dress in cowboy gear for the occasion and watch the rollicking show like other attendees—but they provide real medical care to injured contestants.

Maniilaq Health Center in Alaska serves the health-care needs of Inupiaq Inuit, many of whom live in areas so remote that there are no roads and emergency transportation must be done by air, boat, or snow vehicles.

## Military EMTs

All of the branches of the armed forces—the U.S. Army, Navy, Marines, Air Force, and Coast Guard—employ EMTs. EMTs in the military work on military bases, providing on-site emergency medical care. Each branch of the military employs its own emergency medical service, so ranks and titles differ from service to service. In addition to being trained as soldiers, military EMTs perform the same type of emergency medical procedures as their civilian counterparts. This includes providing airlift and ground ambulance transportation for the wounded, as well as providing emergency medical care as firefighters.

## Volunteer EMTs

For those interested in EMT work but who do not want to pursue it as a full-time job, there is also the option of working as a volunteer EMT. It is sometimes possible to find opportunities as a volunteer EMT at a fire station or private ambulance company, especially in a small town or rural community that may not have the money to hire large numbers of paid EMTs. Often in this situation, you receive on-the-job experience, riding along with others until you learn the job. Working as a volunteer EMT is also a good way to get a feel for what the job is like and learn whether you would really enjoy doing it.

# CHAPTER 6

## Extreme EMR

Some of the common emergencies that EMTs encounter include heart attacks, poisonings, and victims of violence on the street or in the home. However, many EMTs find themselves involved in more extreme emergency situations such as major man-made or natural disasters.

## Major Disasters

The events of September 11, 2001, in New York City, the Washington, D.C., area, and rural Pennsylvania illustrate the nature of heavy urban rescue. The need for this type of service may be the result of massive man-made disasters such as those that occurred at the World Trade Center and the Pentagon.

Major disasters are not restricted to terrorism, however. They can also be the result of technological accidents such as the explosion of a chemical factory, or major transportation accidents such as a train crash. Nor are all major disasters man-made.

Natural disasters like earthquakes, tornadoes, and hurricanes can cause buildings to collapse and vehicles and other heavy objects to trap and injure people. All major disasters, whether the result of acts by people or natural disasters, have certain things in common. Often they have large numbers of victims and require the close cooperation of many different emergency organizations to successfully rescue and treat them.

When this Amtrak train derailed in Kensington, Maryland, 101 people were injured, 6 critically. The EMTs who responded at the scene sent 84 of the injured to area hospitals.

## Who Handles Major Disasters?

The U.S. Department of Health and Human Services (HHS) includes the Office of Emergency Preparedness (OEP). This organization is responsible for coordinating federal health, rescue, medical, and social services groups involved in responding to major disasters, whether natural, technological, or the result of terrorism. It also manages the National Disaster Medical System (NDMS), which is a joint effort of HHS, the Department of Defense (DoD), the Department of Veterans Affairs (VA), the Federal Emergency Management Agency (FEMA), state and local governments, and businesses and volunteers, to provide emergency medical care in the event of a major disaster.

In Canada, the Centre for Emergency Preparedness and Response (CEPR), created in July 2000, is responsible for coordinating the medical response in case of crises such as bioterrorism. It creates emergency medical response plans on a national level for Health Canada, which is the government agency responsible for national health issues.

In addition to federal organizations, American states, provinces in Canada, and local cities and counties maintain emergency disaster response plans.

## Meeting the Challenge: The Disaster Plan

The events of September 11, 2001, were an example of a "multiple casualty incident," according to the Department of

Transportation's EMS standards. A multiple casualty incident is an emergency in which there are many people who must be rescued and treated. This type of event puts an enormous strain on those involved in emergency medical response. They must act in an organized way to save as many people as possible, while at the same time be able to cope with being in danger themselves. This requires that the rescue effort be disciplined and systematic.

The first step in successful large-scale EMR is having a disaster plan—a set of rules and procedures for reacting to an emergency. Such plans let all the members of the EMR team

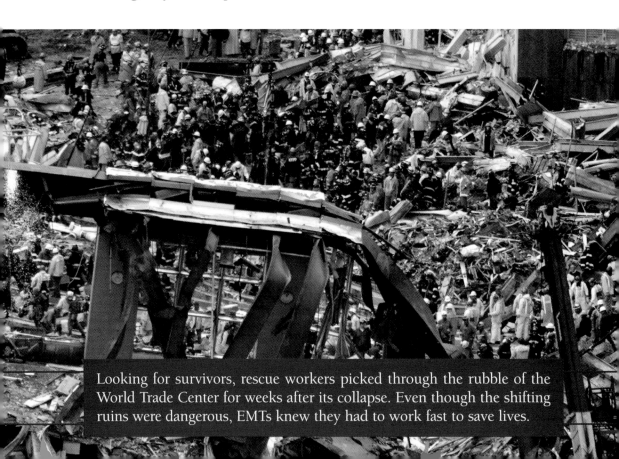

Looking for survivors, rescue workers picked through the rubble of the World Trade Center for weeks after its collapse. Even though the shifting ruins were dangerous, EMTs knew they had to work fast to save lives.

know exactly what they should do, which helps reduce confusion at the scene and makes the team more effective.

An incident commander is designated at any major emergency scene. It is this person's job to assign tasks to other team members. At large disaster sites, where response teams from the fire and police departments and emergency medical services are involved, for instance, it is important that team members from different groups don't waste time performing the same tasks or interfere with each other's rescue efforts. For this reason, a unified command, consisting of personnel from all the agencies involved, is often established.

## Organizing the Rescue Effort

At the site of a major disaster, it is normal to establish specific types of facilities to deal with the various aspects of the rescue operation. These generally include a command center where agency command personnel and communications equipment are located. Sometimes a vehicle specially equipped with communications equipment needed by command personnel is used as a mobile command center that can be moved to any location.

Having a major disaster area clogged with rescue vehicles would make it more difficult for search and rescue teams to do their jobs. To avoid this kind of situation, a staging area is often established. This is a location near enough to the scene of the incident for a vehicle to be brought in in a few minutes, but far enough away so that it does not interfere with rescue efforts at the site. Special areas are also set up for treating and transporting rescued victims. There is often an area where the nature and seriousness of the victims' injuries are evaluated so that they can be transported to the most appropriate medical facilities with the necessary speed. Also, there is often an area for patients awaiting transportation and an area where rescue workers themselves can receive on-site first aid.

## EMR Command in a Major Disaster

In a major medical emergency, individuals from the EMS team are designated to take charge of key responsibilities. These include:

- **Safety officer:** This person is responsible for making sure that EMTs have the right protective gear and are properly identified, as well as for evaluating how dangerous the environment is for EMTs.

- **Triage officer:** "Triage" is French for "sorting" or "classification." The triage officer oversees the personnel who sort the patients according to how seriously they are injured. This allows the most seriously injured to be treated most rapidly.

- **Treatment officer:** This person is responsible for setting up the treatment areas for patients waiting for transportation and supervising the staff who provide treatment.

- **Transport officer:** This person is responsible for organizing the area where ambulances are loaded and, if necessary, arranging for airlift services.

## Future EMR

The need for an effective response to major medical emergencies that result from events like terrorist attacks is greater than ever because of the increased threats of terrorism and the widespread access to weapons that can cause large-scale destruction. Scientists at Sandia National Laboratories (a multiprogram engineering and science laboratory operated by Sandia Corporation, a Lockheed Martin Company, for the U.S. Department of Energy's National Nuclear Security Administration) are asking the question, "What if a bomb or toxic gas were set off in a mall, subway, or other crowded location?" Such events require the coordination of large numbers of personnel from different organizations in order to save as many lives as possible. This is a very complicated task. Many cities and towns, as well as state and federal governments, are creating plans to respond to such disasters. However, there is no chance to practice such a scenario in real life.

The scientists at Sandia may be changing that. They have developed a virtual reality computer simulation to train EMTs and firefighters to respond to large-scale emergencies. The computer program is called BioSimMER. It lets EMTs experience a disaster in a 3-D environment created by the computer. Participants wear goggles and sensors (devices that send a signal to the computer) on their arms, legs, and waist. These devices let them interact with the computer-generated environment.

The environment used is a small airport where a biological warfare agent has been released. Victims with various realistic injuries are scattered around the airport. The EMTs triage, diagnose, and treat the victims using the realistic symptoms of the simulated patients to decide what to do. The EMTs must perform the same steps they use in real life, protecting themselves, evaluating the patients, and using virtual equipment to stabilize and treat the patients. Sandia's program is still a research model, but the scientists are working to make a version that will be available to users in the near future.

## The Need for EMR

No one likes to think about the effects of a major natural disaster or terrorist attack. However, in the event of such an emergency, EMR personnel will be among the key players on the scene. A February 2001 article in *American Medical News* titled "Preparing for the Worst" had this to say: "The need for the medical community to be prepared to deal with terrorism or natural disasters can be likened to the need for automobile insurance: It's something you don't want to use, but when it's needed, there's no real substitute for it." It's hard to disagree with this point. Working in emergency medical response can be demanding and sometimes dangerous, but it is both exciting and a way to make a meaningful difference in people's lives.

# GLOSSARY

**Asclepius**  The Greek god of healing.

**bioterrorism**  The use of a biological substance, such as germs, to kill or injure people with the intent of creating widespread fear and disruption of normal activity.

**Centre for Emergency Preparedness and Response (CEPR)**  The organization responsible for coordinating the emergency medical response to major disasters in Canada.

**CME (continuing medical education)**  A course or workshop taken by medical personnel to improve or update their skills, for which they are given credits. Each type of medical specialty, including EMTs, requires a certain number of CME credits each year to maintain certification.

**CPR (cardiopulmonary resuscitation)**  The process of keeping blood and oxygen circulating in a patient's body when he or she is not breathing or his or her heart has stopped. It may also include procedures to restart the patient's heart.

**EMR (emergency medical response)**  The emergency treatment and transportation of people injured in accidents and disasters.

**EMS (emergency medical services**)  Organizations and individuals that provide on-site urgent medical care and transportation of patients to hospitals.

**EMT**  Emergency medical technician.

**EMT-Basic**  The most basic level of emergency medical technician in the United States.

**EMT-2 and EMT-3**  The intermediate levels of emergency medical technician in the United States; EMT-2s and EMT-3s can perform more advanced procedures than EMT-Basics.

**EMT-Paramedic**  The most advanced level of emergency medical technician in the United States, EMT-Paramedics can use medical monitors and equipment designed to restart people's hearts, as well as administer medication.

**enact**  To make into law.

**Geneva Convention**  A series of international rules governing the conduct of wars.

**Health Canada**  The Canadian government agency responsible for overseeing issues related to health.

**incident commander**  The person in charge of the rescue process at the scene of a major disaster.

**multiple casualty incident**  An emergency in which there are many victims who must be rescued and treated.

**National Disaster Medical System (NDMS)** A joint effort of the U.S. Department of Health and Human Services, the Department of Defense, the Department of Veterans Affairs, the Federal Emergency Management Agency, state and local governments, and businesses and volunteers designed to provide medical assistance in the event of a major disaster.

**Office of Emergency Preparedness (OEP)** The branch of the U.S. Department of Health and Human Services responsible for organizing the response to major disasters.

**protocol** A standard list of instructions detailing the rules and steps for carrying out a particular task.

**sensor** An electronic device that sends signals to and from a computer in response to input such as movement.

**Star of Life** The symbol of emergency medical services, consisting of a six-pointed star composed of three crossed bars with a snake coiled around the center bar.

**virtual reality** A type of computer simulation in which participants wear goggles and sensors that allow them to interact with a computer-generated environment.

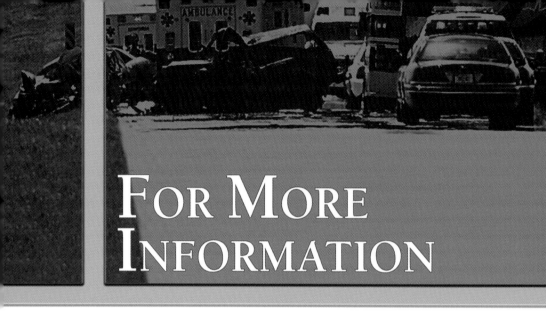

# FOR MORE INFORMATION

American Rescue Team International
P.O. Box 534, Sandia Park
Albuquerque, NM 87047
(505) 281-7977
Web site: http://www.amerrescue.org

Association of Air Medical Services
526 King Street, Suite 415
Alexandria, VA 22314-3143
(703) 836-8732
Web site: http://www.aams.org

Mountain Rescue Association
P.O. Box 501
Poway, CA 92074
(858) 229-4295
Web site: http://www.mra.org

National Association of Emergency Medical Technicians
408 Monroe Street
Clinton, MS 39056-4210
(800) 346-2368
Web site: http://www.naemt.org

National Flight Paramedics Association
383 F Street
Salt Lake City, UT 84103
(800) 381-6372
Web site: http://www.nfpa.rotor.com

National Institute for Urban Search and Rescue
P.O. Box 91648
Santa Barbara, CA 93190
(805) 966-6178
Web site: http://www.niusr.org

## In Canada

Canadian Centre for Emergency Preparedness
1005 Skyview Drive, Suite 202
Burlington, ON L7P 5B1
(905) 319-4031
Web site: http://www.ccep.ca

Paramedic Association of Canada
230 – 1210 Summit Drive, Unit 294
Kamloops, BC V2C 6M1
(250) 314-6416
Web site: http://www.paramedic.ca

## Web Sites

Due to the changing nature of Internet links, the Rosen
Publishing Group, Inc., has developed an online list of Web
sites related to the subject of this book. This site is updated
regularly. Please use this link to access the list:

http://www.rosenlinks.com/csro/emrt/

# FOR FURTHER READING

Canning, Peter. *Rescue 471: A Paramedic's Stories*. New York: Ballantine, 2000.

Hudson, Janice. *Trauma Junkie: Memoirs of an Emergency Flight Nurse*. Buffalo, NY: Firefly Books, 2001.

Katz, Samuel. *Anytime, Anywhere! On Patrol with the NYPD's Emergency Services Unit*. New York: Pocket Books, 1997.

Lafferty, Peter, and David Jefferis. *To The Rescue! The History of Emergency Vehicles*. New York: Franklin Watts, 1990.

Royston, Angela. *Emergency Rescue*. Des Plaines, IL: Heinemann, 1998.

Shapiro, Paul D. *Paramedic*. New York: Bantam, 1998.

Smith, Barry D., Ray Downey, and Jeff Berend. *Rescuers in Action*. St. Louis, MO: Mosby, 1996.

# BIBLIOGRAPHY

Bellis, Mary. "Ambulance History." Retrieved February 12, 2002 (http://inventors.about.com/library/inventors/blambulance.htm).

Canadian Association of Emergency Physicians. "Submission to the Commission on the Future of Health Care in Canada." Retrieved February 12, 2002 (http://www.caep.ca/002.policiies/002-3.romanow/romanow-15.htm).

Davidson, Darren. "The History of Emergency Medicine." Retrieved February 12, 2002 (http://silcon.com/~davidson/ems.html).

D-Net Canada. "Search and Rescue: Canada's National Search-and-Rescue Program—Background Information." Retrieved February 12, 2002 (http://www.dnd.ca/menu/SAR/eng/sar/ginatstar.htm).

Hancock, Cheryl, with Lauren B. Starkey. *EMT Career Starter: Finding and Getting a Great Job.* New York: Learning Express, 2001.

Health Canada. "Backgrounder: Health Canada's Centre for Emergency Preparedness and Response." Retrieved February 12, 2002 (http://www.hc-sc.gc.ca/english/media/releases/2001/2001_110ebk2.htm).

*Journal of Emergency Medical Services.* "Salary Survey 2001." October 2001, pp. 24–33.

Limmer, Daniel, Bob Elling, Michael F. O'Keefe, and Edward T. Dickinson. *Brady Essentials of Emergency Care: A Refresher for the Practicing EMT-B.* Upper Saddle River, NJ: Brady Prentice-Hall, 1999.

Littell, Mary Ann. "First Response to Terror." Retrieved March 29, 2002 (http://www.umdnj.edu/umcweb/hstate/fall01/features/feature02_response.html).

McCarthy, Michael. "Attacks Provide First Major Test of USA's National Antiterrorist Medical Response Plans." *The Lancet.* September 22, 2001, p. 941.

Mountain Rescue Association. "General Information: Some Information on Search and Rescue." Retrieved February 12, 2002 (http://www.mra.org/geninfo.html).

*NNAEMSA News.* "Maniilaq EMS." *NNAEMSA News.* July 2001, p. 5.

Ohio Department of Public Safety Emergency Medical Services Division. "Emergency Medical Services: What EMS Is and How It Began." Retrieved February 12, 2002 (http://www.state.oh.us/odps/division/ems/data/cat7/emswhat.html).

Toronto, City of. "Toronto EMS' History." Retrieved February 12, 2002 (http://www.city.toronto.on.ca/ems/overview/history.htm).

U.S. Department of Labor Bureau of Labor Statistics. "Emergency Medical Technicians and Paramedics." Retrieved February 12, 2002 (http://www.bls.gov/oco/ocos101.htm).

Zatz, Arline. "The Blue 'Star of Life'—The Emergency Medical Care Symbol." Retrieved February 12, 2002 (http://personal.atl.bellsouth.net/lig/m/e/medic119/ems/star.htm).

# INDEX

## ABOUT THE AUTHOR

Jeri Freedman has a B.A. from Harvard University and spent fifteen years working in companies in the biomedical and high-technology fields. She is the author of several plays and, under the name Foxxe, is the coauthor of two science fiction novels. She lives in Boston.

## Photo Credits

Cover © Michal Heron/Corbis; p. 1 © Mark Stehle/AP/Wide World Photos; p. 5 © TimePix; p. 8 © Kathy McLaughlin/ The Image Works; p. 13 © Hulton/Archive/Getty Images; pp. 15, 23 © Corbis; p. 16 © Marc Breault/AP/Wide World Photos; p. 19 © The Image Works; p. 26 © AP/Wide World Photos; p. 30 © John Maniaci/AP/Wide World Photos; p. 34 © Mark E. Gibson/Corbis; p. 36 © Tim Hawkins/Corbis; p. 41 © Andy Miller/Corbis; p. 46 © Kevin Lamarque/TimePix; p. 48 © Mike Segar/TimePix.

## Editor

Annie Sommers

## Designer

Nelson Sá